TAEKWONDO TAEGEUK FORMS

THE OFFICIAL FORMS OF TAEKWONDO

TAEKWONDO TAEGEUK FORMS

THE OFFICIAL FORMS OF TAEKWONDO

BY

SANG H. KIM   *KYU HYUNG LEE*

TURTLE PRESS   SANTA FE

To contact the author or to order additional copies of this book:
    Turtle Press
    PO Box 34010
    Santa Fe NM 87594-4010
    1-800-778-8785
    www.TurtlePress.com

Editor: Cynthia A. Kim
Photos by Marc Yves Regis
Calligraphy by Sang H. Kim

ISBN 9781934903254
LCCN 2011007957
Printed in the United States of America

10 9 8 7 6 5 4 3 2 1 0

Library of Congress Cataloguing in Publication Data

Kim, Sang H.
Taekwondo taegeuk forms : the official forms of taekwondo / by Sang H. Kim, Kyu Hyung Lee.
    p. cm.
ISBN 978-1-934903-25-4
1. Tae kwon do. I. Yi, Kyu-hyong, 1948- II. Title.
GV1114.9.K554 2011
796.815'3--dc22
               2011007957

Contents

TAEGEUK

POOMSAE

Principles of Taegeuk

What is Taegeuk?

The Taegeuk Poomsaes are the official forms required for all color belt students of World Taekwondo Federation affiliated schools or members. Taegeuk is a system of patterns comprised of defensive and offensive techniques used in traditional martial arts. The word "Tae" means "bigness" such as that of the universe and "Geuk" means "infinity" or "ultimate". Thus, "Taegeuk" symbolizes the "Supreme Ultimate" which has no beginning or end but is the origin of everything in the universe.

Taegeuk, or supreme ultimate, refers to the origin from which all life forms arise and to which they return when their lifecycles end. Similarly Taekwondo practice encompasses a complete martial art system, from the most basic elements of fighting skills to advanced levels of philosophical understanding of the relationships between you and your opponent, you and your surroundings, your body and mind, your mind and the universe, winning and losing, fear and joy, and ultimately life and death. All of these components arise from the Taegeuk and occur throughout your life. Thus, Taegeuk is an important concept worthy of further study.

Origin of Taegeuk

The origin of Taegeuk comes from ancient Eastern metaphysics, where two primal opposing yet complementary forces found in all things in the universe. Um, the darker element is passive, feminine, cold and downward seeking; Yang, the brighter element, is active, masculine, warm and upward seeking. If Um represents night, Yang is day.

Nature of Um and Yang

Um and Yang (also known as Yin and Yang) are complementary opposites rather than absolutes: Although Um and Yang are opposing forces, they need and consume each other and work in unity. They each contain a seed of the opposite transforming into the other. Nothing in the universe is totally Um or Yang in nature. Part of Um is in Yang and vice versa.

The qualities of each are not absolute; the opposition is relative and temporary. Um constantly becomes Yang while Yang changes to Um. They are dependent elements with an interdependent nature. Um cannot exist without Yang just as there cannot be night without day.

When Um is excessive, Yang becomes deficient; when Yang becomes dominant, Um weakens. The imbalance makes the energy

Yang   **Um**

level of the weaker more intensely focused, which helps it become stronger in turn. They regain their balance as a pair until one dominates the other again.

The state of balance and unbalance of the two forces constantly transforms themselves through expansion and condensation and fluctuates throughout life. The process of this transformation further divides into Um and Yang producing eight different phenomena called Palgwae.

Palgwae Trigrams from Taegeuk

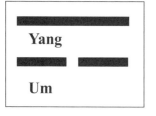

Yang

Um

Palgwae is the by-product of the transformational cycle of the Taegeuk, which in the end returns to Taegeuk. The symbol for Um is a broken bar and for Yang a solid bar. The two divide into the four stages of Um and Yang and further divide into the eight trigrams. From the top of the diagram, the trigrams begin clockwise from Keon (heaven), Sohn (wind), Gam (water), Gahn (mountain), Gon (earth), Jin (thunder), Ri (fire), to Tae (river).

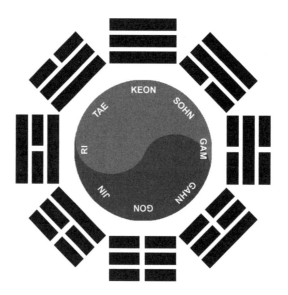

Um and Yang Applied to Poomsae

The opposing phenomena of nature are the main formula of the Taegeuk Poomsae: challenge and response, offense and defense, attack and retreat, fast and slow, hard and soft. An offensive technique must be able to instantly change into a defensive technique. A defensive technique must have offensive readiness.

The keys in practicing the Taegeuk Poomsaes, therefore, are in managing the internal and external energy properly and performing with adequate breath, speed, and power control. Special attention must be given to the transitional techniques, by shifting the center of gravity perpendicular to the ground, in order not to lose the balance. Each technique must be performed with complete focus and dynamic energy.

Symbols for Eight Taegeuk Poomsae

There are eight Taegeuk Poomsaes. Each Poomsae is built upon the previous one, adding more complicated movements, yet every form has unique characteristics and principles that students must adhere to and search for.

Taegeuk Il Jang: Keun meaning heaven: the spirit of solid foundation
Taegeuk Ee Jang: Tae meaning river: inner strength and external gentleness
Taegeuk Sam Jang: Ri meaning fire: the spirit of enthusiasm
Taegeuk Sah Jang: Jin meaning thunder: the spirit of undeniable power and dignity
Taegeuk Oh Jang: Sohn meaning wind: the spirit of gentle power
Taegeuk Yuk Jang: Gam meaning water: the spirit of flow and ultimate flexibility
Taegeuk Chil Jang: Gahn meaning mountain: the spirit of firmness and strength
Taegeuk Pal Jang: Gon meaning earth: the spirit of humbleness

TAEGEUK
IL JANG

KEON

Meaning of Taegeuk Il Jang

The symbol for Taegeuk Il Jang is Keon meaning the sky or heaven, which is the base for the cosmos. It is where everything originates. Thus Taegeuk Il Jang is the most basic form of Taekwondo. This form consists of fundamental movements such as walking stance, front stance, low block, high block, inside block, middle punch, and front kick. It helps a practitioner build a solid base for more complex techniques. This form is for the 8th Gup. There are 18 movements.

Poomsae Line of Taegeuk Il Jang

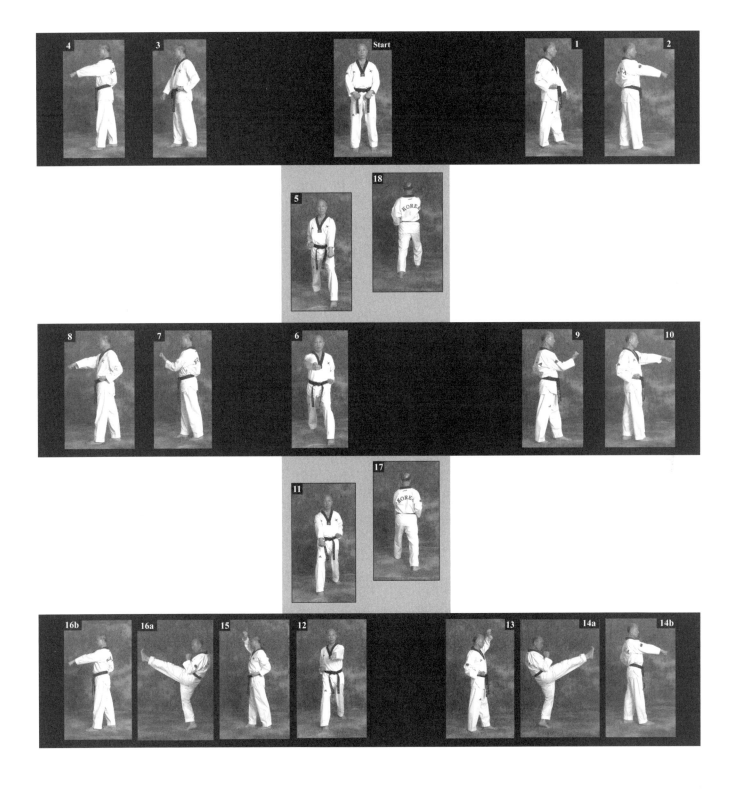

Taegeuk Il Jang

Begin from **ready stance** (junbiseogi), eyes looking forward and feet shoulder width apart.

1. Move the left foot to the left into **left walking stance** (wen apseogi) and execute a **left low section block** (araemakki).

2. Step forward with the right foot into **right walking stance** (oreun apseogi) and execute a **right reverse middle punch** (momtong bandaejireugi).

4. Step forward with the left foot into **left walking stance** (wen apseogi) and execute a **left reverse middle punch** (momtong bandaejireugi).

3. Moving the right foot, turn 180° clockwise to the rear into **right walking stance** (oreun apseogi) and execute a **right low section block** (araemakki).

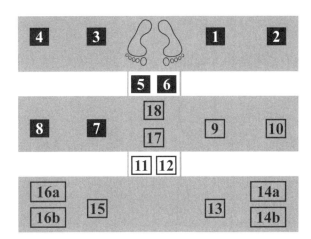

5. Moving the left foot, step 90° to the left into **left front stance** (wen apkubi) and execute a **left low section block** (araemakki).

8. Step forward with the left foot into **left walking stance** (wen apseogi) and execute a **right straight middle punch** (momtong barojireugi).

7. Moving the right foot, step 90° to the right into **right walking stance** (oreun apseogi) and execute a **left inward middle block** (momtong anmakki).

6. Without moving the feet, execute a **right straight middle punch** (momtong barojireugi).

9. Moving the left foot, turn 180° counterclockwise to the rear into **left walking stance** (wen apseogi) and execute a **right inward middle block** (momtong anmakki).

10. Step forward with the right foot into **right walking stance** (oreun apseogi) and execute a **left straight middle punch** (momtong barojireugi).

11. Moving the right foot, step 90° to the right into **right front stance** (oreun apkubi) and execute a **right low section block** (araemakki).

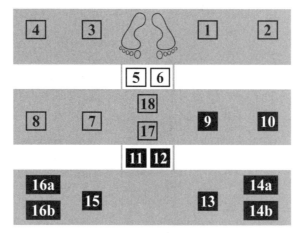

12. Without moving the feet, execute a **left straight middle punch** (momtong barojireugi).

13. Moving the left foot, step 90° to the left into **left walking stance** (wen apseogi) and execute a **left high section block** (olgulmakki).

14a. With the left foot fixed, execute a **right front kick** (oreunbal apchagi).

14b. Set the right foot down in **right walking stance** (oreun apseogi), execute a **right reverse middle punch** (momtong bandaejireugi).

16b. Set the left foot down in **left walking stance** (wen apseogi), execute a **left reverse middle punch** (momtong bandaejireugi).

16a. With the right foot fixed, execute a **left front kick** (wenbal apchagi).

15. Moving the right foot, turn 180° clockwise to the rear into **right walking stance** (oreun apseogi) and execute a **right high section block** (olgulmakki).

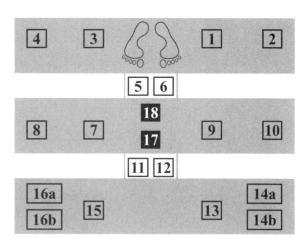

17. Moving the left foot, step 90° to the right into **left front stance** (wen apkubi) and execute a **left low section block** (araemakki).

18. Step forward into **right front stance** (oreun apkubi) and execute a **right reverse middle punch** (momtong bandaejireugi). **Kihap** when punching.

Moving the left foot, return to ready stance by turning 180° counterclockwise.

New Movements in Taegeuk Il Jang

Walking Stance
Apseogi

Walking stance looks like you've stopped walking midstride. The feet are about one stride apart, with their inner edges on one line. The legs are straight and the weight is evenly distributed. The rear foot may turn outward 30° if this is more comfortable.

Front Stance
Apkubi

The feet are about one and a half strides apart. The front foot points forward and the rear foot is turned outward 30°. Bend the front knee so that the shin is perpendicular to the floor. The weight is 2/3 on the front foot. The upper body is slightly angled away from the front.

Low Section Block
Araemakki

When making Araemakki, the fist of the blocking hand first comes up to shoulder level, with the inside of the fist toward the face. When completed, the distance between the blocking fist and the thigh is about 2 fist widths. The other fist rests on the side at belt level.

Inward Middle Block
Momtong Anmakki

When making momtong anmakki, the clenched palm faces forward then snaps toward the centerline. At completion, the elbow is bent slightly less than 90° and the clenched palm faces toward the body.

High Section Block

Olgulmakki

The wrist of the blocking arm passes directly in front of the face and finishes one fist's distance from the forehead. The other fist rests on the side at belt level.

Reverse Middle Punch / Straight Middle Punch

Momtong Bandaejireugi / Momtong Barojireugi

When punching, using the pulling force of the non-punching to generate power. Upon completion, the striking fist is aligned with the solar plexus and the other fist rests on the side at belt level. The target is the solar plexus.

Front Kick

Apchagi

Pull the toes back, striking the target with the ball of the foot. The standing foot may come slightly off the ground but should not fully lift up onto the toes.

TAEGEUK
EE JANG

Meaning of Taegeuk Ee Jang

The symbol of Taegeuk Ee Jang is Tae meaning river which implies internal strength and external gentleness. After diligent practice of Taegeuk Il Jang, now you have a stronger base to develop yourself further. There are more front kicks and block-kick-punch combinations in Taegeuk Ee Jang. Techniques must be performed gently but with dynamic inner power. This form is for the 7th Gup. There are 18 movements.

Poomsae Line of Taegeuk Ee Jang

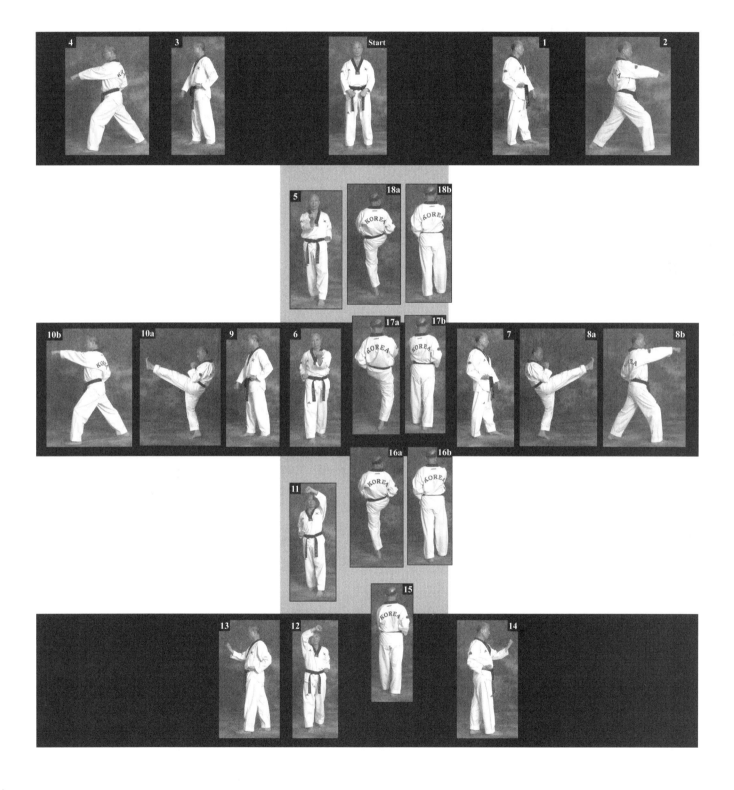

Taegeuk Ee Jang

Begin from **ready stance** (junbiseogi), eyes looking forward and feet shoulder width apart.

1. Move the left foot to the left into **left walking stance** (wen apseogi) and execute a **left low section block** (araemakki).

2. Step forward with the right foot into **right front stance** (oreun apkubi) and execute a **right reverse middle punch** (momtong bandaejireugi).

4. Step forward with the left foot into **left front stance** (wen apkubi) and execute a **left reverse middle punch** (momtong bandaejireugi).

3. Moving the right foot, turn 180° clockwise to the rear into **right walking stance** (oreun apseogi) and execute a **right low section block** (araemakki).

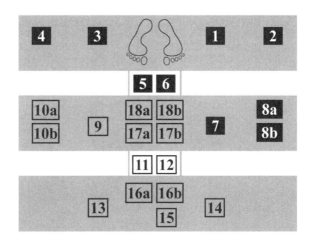

5. Moving the left foot, turn 90° into **left walking stance** (wen apseogi) and execute a **right inward middle block** (momtong anmakki).

6. Step forward with the right foot into **right walking stance** (oreun apseogi) and execute a **left inward middle block** (momtong anmakki).

7. Moving the left foot, turn 90° into **left walking stance** (wen apseogi) and execute a **left low section block** (araemakki).

8a. With the left foot fixed, execute a **right front kick** (oreunbal apchagi).

8b. Set the right foot down in **right front stance** (oreun apkubi), execute a **right high section reverse punch** (olgul bandaejireugi).

11. Moving the left foot, step 90° into **left walking stance** (wen apseogi) and execute a **left high section block** (olgulmakki).

10b. Set the left foot down in **left front stance** (wen apkubi), execute a **left high section reverse punch** (olgul bandaejireugi).

10a. With the right foot fixed, execute a **left front kick** (wenbal apchagi).

9. Moving the right foot, turn 180° clockwise to the rear into **right walking stance** (oreun apseogi) and execute a **right low section block** (araemakki).

12. Stepping forward into **right walking stance** (oreun apseogi) and execute a **right high section block** (olgulmakki).

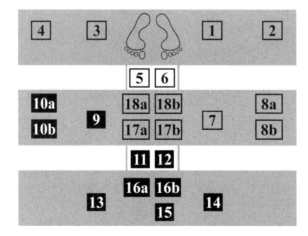

13. Moving the left foot, turn 270° counterclockwise into **left walking stance** (wen apseogi) and execute a **right inward middle block** (momtong anmakki).

14. Sliding the right foot slightly to the right, pivot 180° into **right walking stance** (oreun apseogi) and execute a **left inward middle block** (momtong anmakki).

15. Moving the left foot, step 90° into **left walking stance** (wen apseogi) and execute a **left low section block** (araemakki).

16a. With the left foot fixed, execute a **right front kick** (oreunbal apchagi).

16b. Set the right foot down in **right walking stance** (oreun apseogi), execute a **right reverse middle punch** (momtong bandaejireugi).

17a. With the right foot fixed, execute a **left front kick** (wenbal apchagi).

17b. Set the right foot down in **left walking stance** (wen apseogi), execute a **left reverse middle punch** (momtong bandaejireugi).

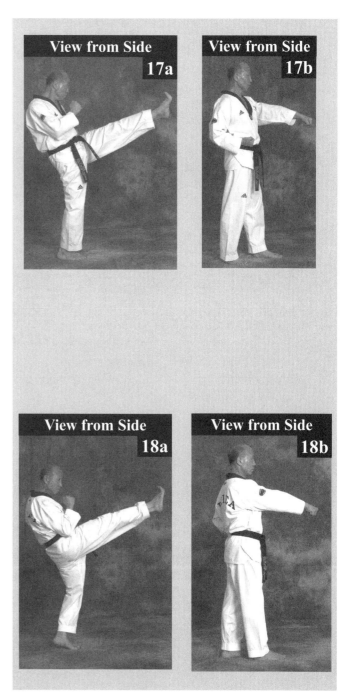

View from Side 17a

View from Side 17b

View from Side 18a

View from Side 18b

18a. With the left foot fixed, execute a **right front kick** (oreunbal apchagi).

18b. Set the right foot down in **right walking stance** (oreun apseogi), execute a **right reverse middle punch** (momtong bandaejireugi) with **Kihap**.

Moving the left foot, return to ready stance by turning 180° counterclockwise.

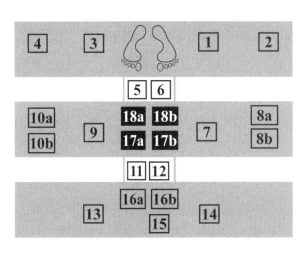

New Movements in Taegeuk Ee Jang

High Section Reverse Punch
Olgul Bandaejireugi
The high section punch is executed like the middle section punch except the target is just below the nose.

TAEGEUK
SAM JANG

Meaning of Taegeuk Sam Jang

The symbol of Taegeuk Sam Jang is Ri meaning fire. Through Taekwondo training, you have developed physical strength, and inner power. At this stage, the more effort you put out, the more your enthusiasm burns. New movements in Taegeuk Sam Jang are back stance, knifehand strike and knifehand block. The block-punch and block-kick combinations require quickness and the ability to coordinate your body to create integral forces. Use speed in defending and power in attacking. This form is for the 6th Gup. There are 20 movements.

Poomsae Line of Taegeuk Sam Jang

Taegeuk Sam Jang

Begin from **ready stance** (junbiseogi), eyes looking forward and feet shoulder width apart.

1. Move the left foot to the left into **left walking stance** (wen apseogi) and execute a **left low section block** (araemakki).

2. With the left foot fixed, execute a **right front kick** (oreunbal apchagi).

4b-c. Set the left foot down in **left front stance** (wen apkubi) and execute a **double punch** (dubeonjireugi), punching with the left hand first then the right.

2b-c. Set the right foot down in **right front stance** (oreun apkubi) and execute a **double punch** (dubeonjireugi), punching with the right hand first then the left.

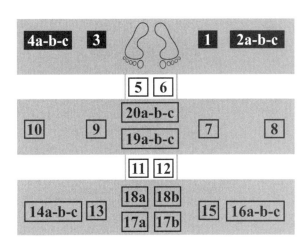

4a. With the right foot fixed, execute a **left front kick** (wenbal apchagi).

3. Moving the right foot, turn 180° clockwise to the rear into **right walking stance** (oreun apseogi) and execute a **right low section block** (araemakki).

5. Moving the left foot, step 90° into **left walking stance** (wen apseogi) and execute a right **inside knifehand strike** (sonnal mokchigi).

6. Stepping forward into **right walking stance** (oreun apseogi), execute a **left inside knifehand strike** (sonnal mokchigi).

7. Moving the left foot, step 90° into **right back stance** (oreun dwitkubi) and execute a **left single knifehand middle section outward block** (hansonnal momtong bakkatmakki).

8. Moving the left foot forward into **left front stance** (wen apkubi), execute a **right straight middle punch** (momtong barojireugi).

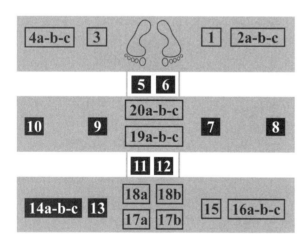

10. Moving the right foot forward into **right front stance** (oreun apkubi), execute a **left straight middle punch** (momtong barojireugi).

9. Sliding the right foot, turn the body 180° clockwise to the rear into **left back stance** (wen dwitkubi) and execute a **right single knifehand middle section outward block** (hansonnal momtong bakkatmakki).

11. Moving the left foot, pivot 90° counterclockwise into **left walking stance** (wen apseogi) and execute a **right inward middle block** (momtong anmakki).

12. Step forward into **right walking stance** (oreun apseogi) and execute a **left inward middle block** (momtong anmakki).

14b-c. Set the right foot down in **right front stance** (oreun apkubi) and execute a **double punch** (dubeonjireugi), punching with the right hand first then the left.

14a. With the left foot fixed, execute a **right front kick** (oreunbal apchagi).

13. Moving the left foot, pivot 270° counterclockwise into **left walking stance** (wen apseogi) and execute a **left low section block** (araemakki).

15. Moving the right foot, turn 180° clockwise into **right walking stance** (oreun apseogi) and execute a **right low section block** (araemakki).

16a. With the right foot fixed, execute a **left front kick** (wenbal apchagi).

16b-c. Set the left foot down in **left front stance** (wen apkubi) and execute a **double punch** (dubeonjireugi), punching with the left hand first then the right.

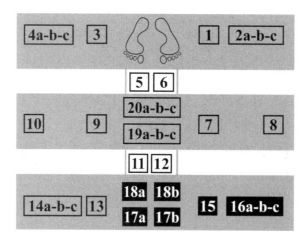

17a. Moving the left foot, step 90° into **left walking stance** (wen apseogi) and execute a **left low section block** (araemakki).

17b. Without moving the feet, immediately execute a **right straight middle punch** (momtong barojireugi).

18a. Step forward into **right walking stance** (oreun apseogi) and execute a **right low section block** (araemakki).

18b. Without moving the feet, immediately execute a **left straight middle punch** (momtong barojireugi).

19a. With the right foot fixed, execute a **left front kick** (wenbal apchagi).

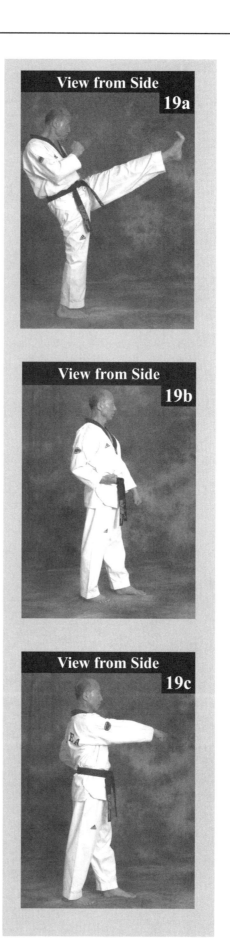

View from Side
19a

19b. Set the left foot down in **left walking stance** (wen apseogi) and execute a **left low section block** (araemakki).

View from Side
19b

19c. Without moving the feet, immediately execute a **right straight middle punch** (momtong barojireugi).

View from Side
19c

20a. With the left foot fixed, execute a **right front kick** (oreunbal apchagi).

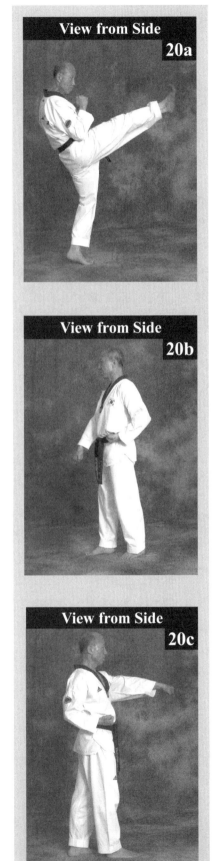

20b. Set the left foot down in **right walking stance** (oreun apseogi) and execute a **right low section block** (araemakki).

20c. Without moving the feet, immediately execute a **left straight middle punch** (momtong barojireugi) with **Kihap**.

Moving the left foot, return to ready stance by turning counterclockwise.

New Movements in Taegeuk Sam Jang

Double Punch
Dubeonjireugi
The double punch is performed by executing two punches in rapid succession, first punching with the front hand and then with the rear hand. The target for both punches is the solar plexus.

Single Knifehand Middle Section Outward Block
Hansonnal Momtong Bakkatmakki
The front hand forms a blade with the wrist straight. The rear hand forms a fist at belt level. Two thirds of the weight is on the rear leg and one third is on the front leg.

Straight Middle Punch
Momtong Barojireugi
Performed in the same way as a middle punch except the punch is executed with the rear hand. The target is the solar plexus.

Inside Knifehand Strike
Sonnal Mokchigi
The striking knife hand travels from out to in while twisting the forearm. The force is maximized by snapping at impact.

Back Stance
Dwitkubi
The rear foot points outward at a 90° angle and the front foot points straight forward. The front foot is about one stride from the rear foot and the heels are aligned. The knees are bent about 60 -70 degrees. The weight is about two thirds on the rear foot.

TAEGEUK
SAH JANG

Meaning of Taegeuk Sah Jang

The symbol of Taegeuk Sah Jang is Jin meaning thunder, undeniable power and dignity. As the power comes from the concentrated energy, the actions in the form must be dynamic and focused. There are more advanced movements in this Poomsae such as double knifehand block, fingertip thrust, swallow stance knifehand strike, consecutive side kicks, and cross stance back fist. To prepare for Kyorugi practice, there are more transitional movements to help you improve body shifting and coordination. This is for the 5th Gup. There are 20 movements.

Poomsae Line of Taegeuk Sah Jang

Taegeuk Sah Jang

Begin from **ready stance** (junbiseogi), eyes looking forward and feet shoulder width apart.

1. Move the left foot to the left into **right back stance** (oreun dwitkubi) and execute a **double knifehand block** (sonnal momtongmakki).

2. Step forward with the right foot into **right front stance** (oreun apkubi) and execute a **right vertical fingertip thrust** (pyonsonkkeut sewotzireugi).

4	3		1	2

	5	6		
15	20a-b-c		18	
16	19a-b-c		17	

	7	8		

| 10a | | 14a | 14b | | 12a |
| 10b | 9 | 13 | | 11 | 12b |

4. Step forward with the left foot into **left front stance** (wen apkubi) and execute a **left vertical fingertip thrust** (pyonsonkkeut sewotzireugi).

3. Moving the right foot, turn 180° clockwise to the rear into **left back stance** (wen dwitkubi) and execute a **double knifehand block** (sonnal momtongmakki).

5. Moving the left foot, turn 90° into **left front stance** (wen apkubi) and execute a **swallow form knifehand strike** (jebipoom mokchigi).

6a. With the left foot fixed, execute a **right front kick** (oreunbal apchagi).

6b. Step down into **right front stance** (oreun apkubi) and execute a **left straight middle punch** (momtong barojireugi).

7. Pivoting on the right foot, execute a **left side kick** (wenbal yopchagi).

8a. Pivoting on the left foot, execute a **right side kick** (oreunbal yopchagi).

8b. Set the right foot down in **left back stance** (wen dwitkubi), execute a **double knifehand block** (sonnal momtongmakki).

10b. Return the right foot to its original position in **right back stance** (oreun dwitkubi) and execute a **right inward middle block** (momtong anmakki).

10a. With the left foot fixed, execute a **right front kick** (oreun apchagi).

9. Moving the right foot, turn 270° counterclockwise into **right back stance** (oreun dwitkubi) and execute a **left outward middle block** (momtong bakkatmakki).

11. Pivoting the body 180° clockwise into **left back stance** (wen dwitkubi), execute a **right outward middle block** (momtong bakkatmakki).

12a. With the right foot fixed, execute a **left front kick** (wen apchagi).

12b. Return the left foot to its original position in **left back stance** (wen dwitkubi) and execute a **left inward middle block** (momtong anmakki).

14b. Step down into **right front stance** (oreun apkubi) and execute a **right backfist strike** (deungjumeok apchigi).

14a. With the left foot fixed, execute a **right front kick** (oreun apchagi).

13. Moving the left foot, turn 90° counterclockwise into **left front stance** (wen apkubi) and execute a **swallow form knifehand strike** (jebipoom mokchigi).

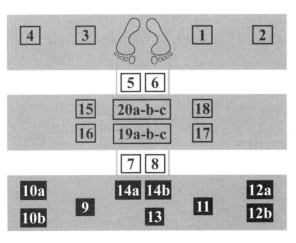

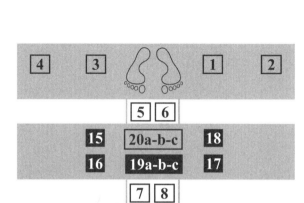

16. Without moving the feet execute a **right straight middle punch** (momtong barojireugi).

15. Moving the left foot, turn 90° counterclockwise into **left walking stance** (wen apseogi) and execute a **left inward middle block** (momtong anmakki).

17. Pivoting the body 180° clockwise into **right walking stance** (oreun apseogi), execute a **right inward middle block** (momtong anmakki).

18. Without moving the feet execute a **left straight middle punch** (momtong barojireugi).

19b-c. Without moving the feet, execute a **double punch** (dubeonjireugi), punching with the right hand first then the left.

19a. Moving the left foot, turn 90° counterclockwise into **left front stance** (wen apkubi) and execute a **left inward middle block** (momtong anmakki).

Moving the left foot, return to ready stance by turning counterclockwise.

20b-c. Without moving the feet, execute a **double punch** (dubeonjireugi), punching with the left hand first then the right.

20a. Step forward into **right front stance** (oreun apkubi) and execute a **right inward middle block** (momtong anmakki).

New Movements in Taegeuk Sah Jang

Double Knifehand Block

Sonnal Momtongmakki

The fingertips of the front hand are held at shoulder height, with the wrist straight and the palm facing front. The wrist of the supporting hand is aligned with the solar plexus, but not resting on the body.

Outward Middle Block

Momtong Bakkatmakki

The fist of the blocking arm should be held in line with the shoulder both vertically and horizontally. The other fist rests on the side at belt level.

Middle Block

Momtongmakki

The fist of the blocking arm is aligned with the center of the body, at shoulder height. The elbow is bent 90° to 120° and the wrist should not be bent. The other fist rests on the side at belt level.

Backfist Strike

Deungjumeok apchigi

The backfist strikes with the first and second knuckles. The target is the face, just below the nose. Turn the upper body about 45° away from the front. Pull the striking fist directly under the opposite armpit when performing the strike.

Vertical Fingertip Thrust

Pyonsonkkeut Sewotzireugi

The supporting hand performs a pressing block, with the hand open and the palm facing downward. The striking hand rests on the knuckles of the blocking hand. The target for the fingertip strike is the solar plexus. Keep the wrist and fingers of the striking hand straight and fold the thumb down onto the palm.

Swallow Form Knifehand Strike

Jebipoom Mokchigi

The front hand is held just above the forehead in a high section knifehand block. The rear hand executes a knifehand strike to the neck. Keep both wrists straight and fully extend the striking arm, twisting the upper body and hips into the strike.

Side Kick

Yopchagi

Begin the side kick by lifting the kicking leg, bending the knee then turning to the side. Once the body is facing sideways, pivot the supporting foot (on the ball of the foot) fully away from the direction of the target and extend the leg to kick. Strike the target with the foot blade and heel. The head and upper body should be raised so the body forms a Y shape at the pinnacle of the kick. The eyes should be on the target, which is the face or solar plexus.

TAEGEUK
OH JANG

SOHN

Meaning of Taegeuk Oh Jang

The symbol of Taegeuk Oh Jang is Sohn meaning the wind. The wind is so gentle when it is a breeze and devastating when it becomes a hurricane. Human power can also be used either way. Taegeuk Oh Jang is designed to develop the inner energy and kinetic force of the body with the application of the two opposite phenomena of nature. New movements are hammer fist, elbow strike, sidekick with side punch, and jumping cross stance. Special attention should be paid to striking a specific target area with the elbow. This form is for the 4th Gup. There are 20 movements.

Poomsae Line of Taegeuk Oh Jang

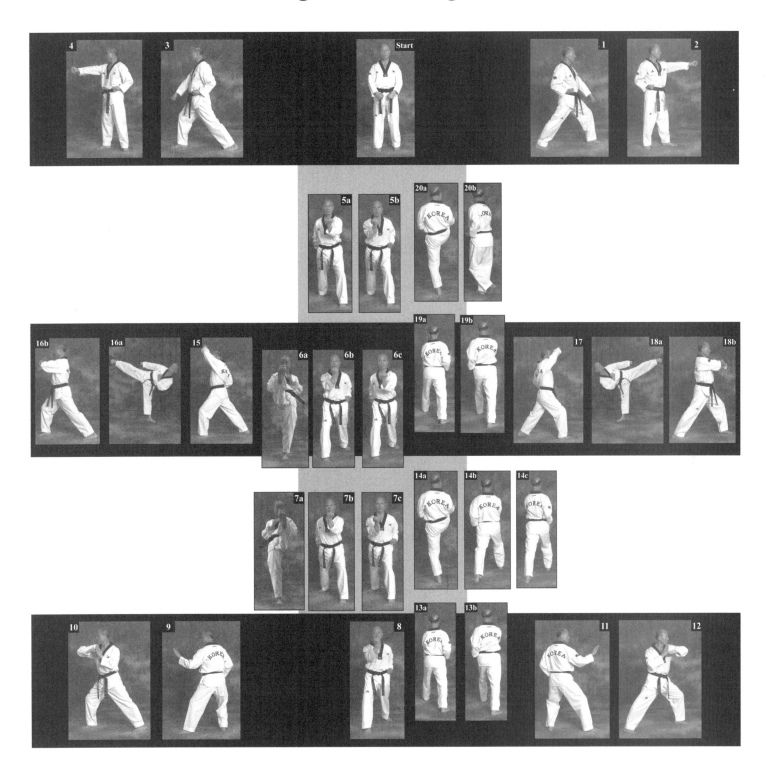

Taegeuk Oh Jang

Begin from **ready stance** (junbiseogi), eyes looking forward and feet shoulder width apart.

1. Move the left foot to the left into **left front stance** (wen apkubi) and execute a **left low section block** (araemakki).

2. Draw the left foot toward the right foot into **left stance** (wenseogi) and execute a **left downward hammerfist strike** (mejumeok naeryochigi).

4. Draw the right foot toward the left foot into **right stance** (oreunseogi) and execute a **right downward hammerfist strike** (mejumeok naeryochigi).

3. Turn to the right into **right front stance** (oreun apkubi) and execute a **right low section block** (araemakki).

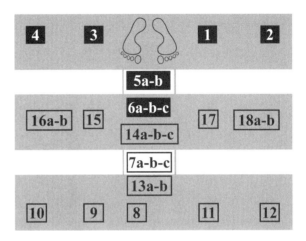

5a. Moving the left foot, turn 90° into **left front stance** (wen apkubi) and execute a **left inward middle block** (momtong anmakki).

5b. With the feet fixed, immediately execute a **right inward middle block** (momtong anmakki).

6a. With the left foot fixed, execute a **right front kick** (oreunbal apchagi).

6b. Set the right foot down in **right front stance** (oreun apkubi) and execute a **right backfist** (deungjumeok apchigi).

6c. With the feet fixed, immediately execute a **left inward middle block** (momtong anmakki).

7a. With the right foot fixed, execute a **left front kick** (wenbal apchagi).

7b. Set the left foot down in **left front stance** (wen apkubi) and execute a **left backfist** (deungjumeok apchigi).

7c. With the feet fixed, immediately execute a **right inward middle block** (momtong anmakki).

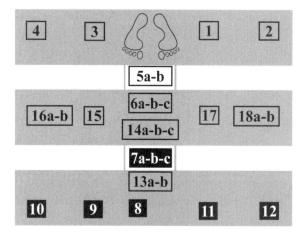

8. Step forward into **right front stance** (oreun apkubi) and execute a **right backfist** (deungjumeok apchigi).

10. Step forward into **right front stance** (oreun abkubi) and execute a **right inward elbow strike** (palkup dollyochigi).

9. Moving the left foot, turn 270° counterclockwise into **right back stance** (oreun dwitkubi) and execute a **single knifehand middle section outward block** (hansonnal momtong bakkatmakki).

11. Moving the right foot, turn 180° into **left back stance** (wen dwitkubi) and execute a **single knifehand middle section outward block** (hansonnal momtong bakkatmakki).

12. Step forward into **left front stance** (wen abkubi) and execute a **left inward elbow strike** (palkup dollyochigi).

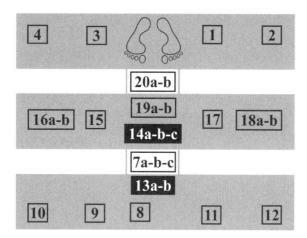

13b. Without moving the feet, execute a **right inward middle block** (momtong anmakki).

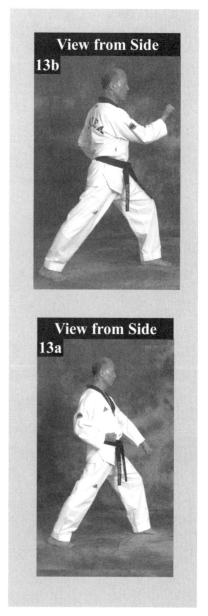

13a. Moving the left foot, turn 90° into **left front stance** (wen apkubi) and execute a **left low section block** (araemakki).

14c. Without moving the feet, execute a **left inward middle block** (momtong anmakki).

14b. Set the right foot down in **right front stance** (oreun apkubi) and execute a **right low section block** (araemakki).

14a. With the left foot fixed, execute a **right front kick** (oreunbal apchagi).

16b. Set the right foot down into **right front stance** (oreun apkubi) and execute a **left elbow target strike** (palkup pyojeokchigi).

16a. Pivoting on the left foot, execute a **right side kick** (oreunbal yopchagi).

15. Moving the left foot, turn 90° counterclockwise into **left front stance** (wen apkubi) and execute a **left high section block** (ogulmakki).

17. Moving the right foot, turn 180° clockwise into **right front stance** (oreun apkubi) and execute a **right high section block** (ogulmakki).

18a. Pivoting on the right foot, execute a **left side kick** (wenbal yopchagi).

18b. Set the left foot down into **left front stance** (wen apkubi) and execute a **right elbow target strike** (palkup pyojeokchigi).

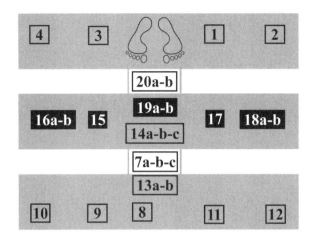

19b. Without moving the feet, execute a **right inward middle block** (momtong anmakki).

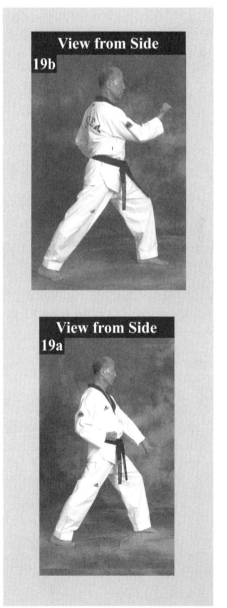

19a. Moving the left foot, turn 90° into **left front stance** (wen apkubi) and execute a **left low section block** (araemakki).

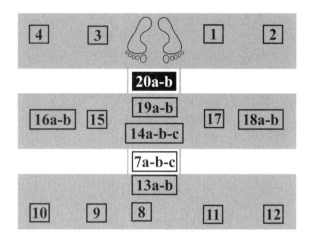

Moving the left foot, return to ready stance by turning counterclockwise.

20b. Before setting the right foot down, jump forward a step landing in **rear cross stance** (dwi koaseogi) and execute a **backfist strike** (deungjumeok apchigi) with **Kihap**.

20a. With the left foot fixed, execute a **right front kick** (oreunbal apchagi).

New Movements in Taegeuk Oh Jang

Left or Right Stance

Wenseogi or Oreunseogi

From ready stance, turn the right foot outward 90° for right stance or the left foot outward 90° for left stance. This stance is used for hammerfist and backfist techniques in the Taegeuk Poomsae.

Rear Cross Stance

Dwi Koaseogi

When making cross stance, the front foot lands hard (pounding the ground), with the rear foot immediately following. The toes of the rear foot are placed beside the blade of the front foot and the right calf touches the left in an X formation. Both knees are bent.

Inward Elbow Strike

Palkup Dollyochigi

The elbow is held just above shoulder height and aligned with the front shoulder. The fist faces the floor and is held slightly away from the body. Turn the upper body into the strike.

Elbow Target Strike

Palkup Pyojeokchigi

To execute the elbow target strike, first stretch the target hand out, arm straight and hand open. Strike the elbow into the target hand, rather than slapping the target hand against the elbow. Keep the target hand open and do not place the thumb on the elbow.

Downward Hammerfist Strike

Mejumeok Naeryochigi

In an in-to-out circular motion, strike vertically downward with the soft side of the clenched fist. At completion, the arm should be parallel to the floor. In Taegeuk Oh Jang, the fist is aligned with the inside edge of the chest.

TAEGEUK
YUK JANG

Meaning of Taegeuk Yuk Jang

The symbol for Taegeuk Yuk Jang is Gam meaning water, the sustenance of life. Water symbolizes a constant flow and the ultimate flexibility. Not only must the techniques flow like water but the mind must be flexible as well. New techniques are single knifehand high section block, roundhouse kick, and palm heel pressing block. Special attention must be paid to the foot position right after executing the two roundhouse kicks. This form is for the 3rd Gup. There are 19 movements.

Poomsae Line of Taegeuk Yuk Jang

Taegeuk Yuk Jang

Begin from **ready stance** (junbiseogi), eyes looking forward and feet shoulder width apart.

1. Move the left foot to the left into **left front stance** (wen apkubi) and execute a **left low section block** (araemakki).

2a. With the left foot fixed, execute a **right front kick** (oreunbal apchagi).

2b. Set the right foot down in **right back stance** (oreun dwitkubi) and execute a **left outward middle block** (momtong bakkatmakki)

4b. Set the left foot down in **left back stance** (wen dwitkubi) and execute a **right outward middle block** (momtong bakkatmakki).

4a. With the right foot fixed, execute a **left front kick** (wenbal apchagi).

3. Turn to the right into **right front stance** (oreun apkubi) and execute a **right low section block** (araemakki).

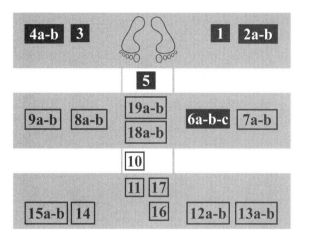

5. Moving the left foot, turn 90° into **left front stance** (wen apkubi) and execute a **right single knifehand twist block** (hansonnal bitureomakki).

6a. Pivoting on the left foot, execute a **right high section roundhouse kick** (oreunbal olgul dollyochagi).

6b. Set the right foot down in front, then turn 90° to the left into **left front stance** (wen apkubi) and execute a **left high section outward block** (olgul bakkatmakki).

6c. With the feet fixed, immediately execute a **right straight middle punch** (momtong barojireugi).

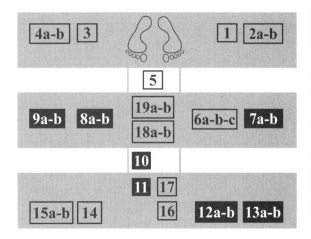

7a. With the left foot fixed, execute a **right front kick** (oreunbal apchagi).

7b. Set the right foot down in **right front stance** (oreun apkubi) and execute a **left straight middle punch** (momtong barojireugi).

9b. Set the left foot down in **left front stance** (wen apkubi) and execute a **right straight middle punch** (momtong barojireugi).

9a. With the right foot fixed, execute a **left front kick** (wenbal apchagi).

8b. With the feet fixed, immediately execute a **left straight middle punch** (momtong barojireugi).

8a. Moving the right foot, turn 180° counterclockwise into **right front stance** (oreun apkubi) and execute a **right high section outward block** (olgul bakkatmakki).

10. Moving the left foot, turn 90° counterclockwise into **parallel stance** (naranhiseogi) and execute a **low section opening block** (arae hechomakki).

11. Moving the right foot, step forward into **right front stance** (oreun apkubi) and execute a **left single knifehand twist block** (hansonnal bitureomakki).

12a. Pivoting on the right foot, execute a **left high section roundhouse kick** (wenbal olgul dollyochagi) with **kihap**.

12b. Set the left foot down in front, then turn 270° counterclockwise (moving the right foot) into **right front stance** (oreun apkubi) and execute a **right low section block** (araemakki).

13a. With the right foot fixed, execute a **left front kick** (wenbal apchagi).

13b. Set the left foot down in **left back stance** (wen dwitkubi) and execute a **right outward middle block** (momtong bakkatmakki).

15b. Set the right foot down in **right back stance** (oreun dwitkubi) and execute a **left outward middle block** (momtong bakkatmakki).

15a. With the left foot fixed, execute a **right front kick** (oreunbal apchagi).

14. Moving the left foot, turn 180° counterclockwise into **left front stance** (wen apkubi) and execute a **left low section block** (araemakki).

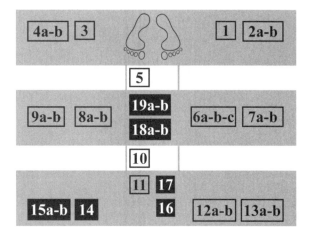

16. Moving the right foot, turn 90° counterclockwise into **right back stance (**oreun dwitkubi) and execute a **double knifehand block** (sonnal momtongmakki).

17. Moving the left foot, step backward into **left back stance** (wen dwitkubi) and execute a **double knifehand block** (sonnal momtongmakki).

19a. Moving the left foot, step backward into **right front stance** (oreun apkubi) and execute a **right palm heel middle section block** (oreun batangson momtongmakki).

19b. With the feet fixed, immediately execute a **left straight middle punch** (momtong barojireugi).

Moving the left foot, return to ready stance by stepping forward.

18a. Moving the right foot, step backward into **left front stance** (wen apkubi) and execute a **left palm heel middle section block** (wen batangson momtongmakki).

18b. With the feet fixed, immediately execute a **right straight middle punch** (momtong barojireugi).

New Movements in Taegeuk Yuk Jang

Parallel Stance
Naranhiseogi
The feet are one foot's width apart and parallel to each other. The legs are straight and the weight is evenly distributed.

Single Knifehand Twist Block
Hansonnal Bitureomakki
The rear hand forms a blade with the wrist straight. The front hand forms a fist at belt level. Two thirds of the weight is on the front leg and one third is on the rear leg. The upper body twists against the block to add power.

High Section Outward Block
Olgul Bakkatmakki
The wrist of the blocking arm passes directly in front of the face and finishes just outside the body. The other fist rests on the side at belt level.

Palm Heel Middle Section Block
Batangson Momtongmakki
The palm is turned parallel to the chest with the fingertips pointing upward. The other fist rests on the side at belt level.

Low Section Opening Block

Arae Hechomakki

When making low section opening block, use a slow controlled movement, exhaling forcefully for the duration of the execution. Look straight ahead throughout the movement.

High Section Roundhouse Kick

Olgul Dollyochagi

Transfer the weight to the pivot foot and immediately chamber the kicking leg and pivot on the ball of the foot. Strike the target with the ball of the foot or the instep. Stop the foot at the target and retract along the same path; do not follow through the target.

TAEGEUK
CHIL JANG

GAHN

Meaning of Taegeuk Chil Jang

The symbol of Taegeuk Chil Jang is Gahn meaning mountain. A mountain is the spirit of firmness and strength. At this level the practitioner's dedication to training starts firmly rooting in the heart. The meaning of self-improvement through Taekwondo becomes deeper daily. Therefore, it is recommended that you reexamine all of the learned skills so that the foundation of skills is strongly secured. You may experience some difficulties and obstacles mentally and physically. Effort is required to get through this stage. New techniques are double knifehand low section block, scissors block, knee strike, middle section opening block, cross block, side punch, tiger stance and horseriding stance. Powerful and articulate execution is required in single movements and smooth transitions are necessary in combination techniques. This form is for the 2nd Gup. There are 25 movements.

Poomsae Line of Taegeuk Chil Jang

Taegeuk Chil Jang

Begin from **ready stance** (junbiseogi), eyes looking forward and feet shoulder width apart.

1. Move the left foot to the left into **left tiger stance** (wen beomseogi) and execute a **right palm heel middle section block** (batangson momtongmakki).

2a. With the left foot fixed, execute a **right front kick** (oreunbal apchagi).

2b. Set the right foot down in **left tiger stance** (wen beomseogi) and execute a **left inward middle block** (momtong anmakki).

4b. Set the left foot down in **right tiger stance** (oreun beomseogi) and execute a **right inward middle block** (momtong anmakki).

4a. With the right foot fixed, execute a **left front kick** (wenbal apchagi).

3. Turn to the right into **right tiger stance** (oreun beomseogi) and execute a **left palm heel middle section block** (batangson momtongmakki).

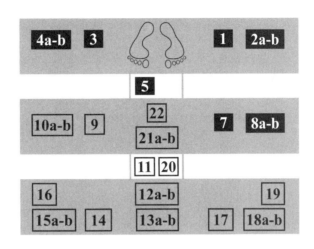

5. Moving the left foot, turn 90° into **right back stance** (oreun dwitkubi) and execute a **left double knifehand low section block** (sonnal arraemakki).

6. Moving the right foot, step forward into **left back stance** (wen dwitkubi) and execute a **right double knifehand low section block** (sonnal arraemakki).

7. Moving the left foot, turn 90° clockwise into **left tiger stance** (wen beomseogi) and execute an **augmented palm heel inward middle section block** (batangson kodureo momtong anmakki).

8a-b. With the feet fixed, twist the upper body to execute a **right backfist strike** (deungjumeok apchigi).

8a-b. With the feet fixed, twist the upper body to execute a **left backfist strike** (deungjumeok apchigi).

9. Pivot 180° clockwise into **right tiger stance** (oreun beomseogi) and execute an **augmented palm heel inward middle section block** (batangson kodureo momtong anmakki).

11. Turning 90° counterclockwise, draw the left foot to the right foot, making **close stance** (moaseogi). Execute a **covered fist** (bojumeok).

12a-b. Step forward with the left foot into **left front stance** (wen apkubi) and execute a **scissors block** (kawimakki).

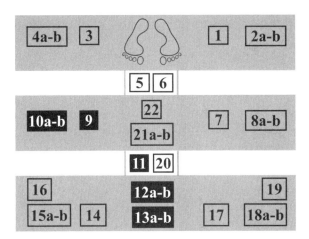

13a-b. Step forward with the right foot into **right front stance** (oreun apkubi) and execute a **scissors block** (kawimakki).

16. With the right foot fixed, step the left foot back into **right front stance** (oreun apkubi) and execute a **low section cross block** (otkoreo araemakki).

15b. Jump forward into **left rear cross stance** (wenbal dwi koaseogi) and execute a **double uppercut** (dujumeok jecheojireugi).

15a. With the left foot fixed, open the hands then execute a **right knee strike** (oreunbal mureupchigi). As you pull downward into the strike, clench the fists.

17. Moving the right foot, turn 180° clockwise into **right front stance** (oreun apkubi) and execute a **middle section opening block** (momtong hechomakki).

18a. With the right foot fixed, open the hands then execute a **left knee strike** (wenbal mureupchigi). As you pull downward into the strike, clench the fists.

17b. Jump forward into **right rear cross stance** (oreunbal dwi koaseogi) and execute a **double uppercut** (dujumeok jecheojireugi).

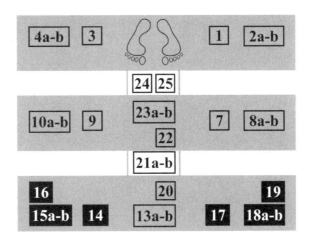

14. Moving the left foot, turn 270° counterclockwise into **left front stance** (wen apkubi) and execute a **middle section opening block** (momtong hechomakki).

19. With the left foot fixed, step the right foot back into **left front stance** (wen apkubi) and execute a **low section cross block** (otkoreo araemakki).

21b. Stepping down into **horseriding stance** (juchumseogi), execute a **right elbow target strike** (oreunpalkup pyojeokchigi).

View from Side

21b

View from Side

21a

View from Side

20

21a. Without moving the left foot, execute a **right target kick** (pyojeokchagi).

20. Moving the left foot, turn 90° counterclockwise into **left walking stance** (wen apseogi) and execute a **left outward backfist strike** (deungjumeok bakkatchigi).

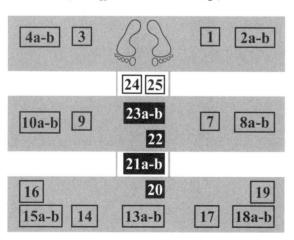

23b. Stepping down
into **horseriding stance**
(juchumseogi), execute a **left
elbow target strike** (wenpalkup
pyojeokchigi).

23a. Without moving the right
foot, execute a **left target kick**
(pyojeokchagi).

22. With the right foot fixed, draw the
left foot slightly forward into **right
walking stance** (oreun apseogi) and
execute a **right outward backfist
strike** (deungjumeok bakkatchigi).

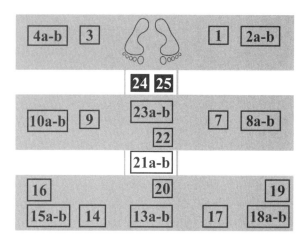

Moving the left foot, return to ready stance.

25. Pulling the opponent with the left hand, step forward with the right foot into **horseriding stance** (juchumseogi) and execute a **right middle section side punch** (momtong yopjireugi) with **kihap**.

24. With the feet fixed, execute a **left single knifehand middle section side block** (wen hansonnal momtong yopmakki).

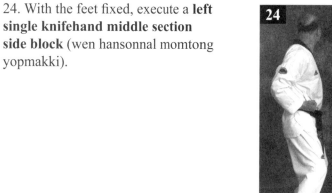

New Movements in Taegeuk Chil Jang

Tiger stance

Beomseogi

From close stance, move one foot about a foot's length forward and turn the other foot outward 30°. The weight is entirely on the rear foot and the muscles of the abdomen are tensed. The knees should be aligned with the toes when looking down at the feet.

Close Stance

Moaseogi

Stand upright with the feet touching and the knees straight. Tighten your Danjun and relax your shoulders. Tuck in your chin.

Horseriding Stance

Juchumseogi

The feet are approximately two feet apart with the soles parallel to each other. Bend the knees to about 120° and pull them inward. Spread the weight evenly between both feet and focus it inward, tensing the muscles of the abdomen.

Double Knifehand Low Section Block

Sonnal Arraemakki

The front hand is held about 2 fists' distance from the front thigh, parallel to the surface of the thigh. The supporting hand is held in front of the solar plexus but does not touch the body. The wrists should be straight.

Augmented Palm Heel Inward Middle Section Block

Batangson Kodureo Momtong Anmakki

Bring the augmented fist under the elbow of the blocking arm with the blocking palm facing inward. Keep the thumb of the blocking hand bent.

Middle Section Opening Block

Momtong Hechomakki

Middle section opening block is two simultaneous outward middle blocks. The wrists should be positioned no wider than the shoulders.

Scissors Block

Kawimakki

One hand makes low block and the other makes outward middle block. While making scissors block, the arms should cross in front of the chest and the hands should arrive at the stopping points simultaneously.

Low Section Cross Block

Otkoreo Arraemakki

The wrists are crossed and the palms face outward. When executing low section cross block, both fists are raised to the side of the rear foot and the block is delivered from the centerline of the body. The arm on the same side as the front leg is always on the bottom.

Single Knifehand Middle Section Side Block

Hansonnal Momtong Yopmakki

Align the tip of the knifehand with the line of the shoulders. Keep the back of the hand wrist and forearm straight with the arm bent approximately 90°. Position the other hand at belt level.

Covered Fist

Bojumeok

Cover the right fist with the left hand. Position the hands just below chin-height, with the elbows tucked within the vertical line of the shoulders.

Outward Backfist Strike

Deungjumeok Bakkatchigi

Strike outward using the two major knuckles. Align the fist with the height of the shoulder. Position the other hand at belt level.

Middle Section Side Punch

Momtong Yopjireugi

From the waist, execute the punch to the side, with the fist ending at shoulder height. The eyes are looking in the same direction as the punch and the body is turned sideways.

Double Uppercut

Dujumeok Jecheojireugi

From the waist, snap both fists upward. At completion, the fists should be aligned with each other, just below shoulder height. Tuck the elbows in close to the trunk.

Knee Strike

Mureupchigi

Bring the knee upward, with the toes pointed and the ankle drawn toward the thigh. Simultaneously bring the hands downward to offset the reaction force of the knee strike.

Target Kick

Pyojeokchagi

Place the target hand at the intended position and slap the palm with the instep. The position of the target hand should remain fixed; do not move the hand to meet the foot.

TAEGEUK
PAL JANG

Meaning of Taegeuk Pal Jang

The symbol of Taegeuk Pal Jang is Kohn meaning earth, which is the foundation of growth for all life and the place to which all life returns. Taegeuk Pal Jang is the last Poomsae before becoming a black belt. This end is a new beginning. Perfection of all basic Taekwondo skills and maturity of character are the goals at this stage. If pride, confidence, and dignity are the results of training, honesty and humbleness are prerequisites for the black belt stage. Students must perfect Taegeuk Il Jang through Taegeuk Pal Jang to be eligible to apply for First Dan black belt. New techniques are jump front kick, single mountain block, and uppercut. Accurate footwork is necessary for the combinations in Taegeuk Pal Jang. This form is required for the 1st Gup. There are 27 movements.

Poomsae Line of Taegeuk Pal Jang

Taegeuk Pal Jang

Begin from **ready stance** (junbiseogi), eyes looking forward and feet shoulder width apart.

1. Moving the left foot, step forward into **right back stance** (oreun dwitkubi) and execute an **augmented outward middle section block** (kodureo momtong bakkatmakki).

2. Sliding the left foot forward into **left front stance** (wen apkubi), execute a **right straight middle punch** (momtong barojireugi).

3a. Begin executing a **double front kick** (dubal dangseong apchagi) by jumping with a **right front kick** (oreunbal apchagi).

3b. Follow immediately with a higher jumping **left front kick** (wenbal apchagi) with **kihap** to complete the double kick.

3c. Land two steps forward in **left front stance** (wen apkubi) and execute a **left inward middle block** (momtong anmakki).

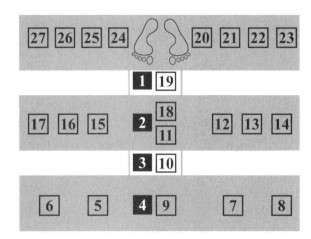

3d-e. With the feet fixed, execute a **double punch** (momtong dubeonjireugi), punching first with the right hand and then with the left.

4. Step forward with the right foot into **right front stance** (oreun apkubi) and execute a **right reverse middle punch** (momtong bandaejireugi).

6. Without stepping, slowly pivot into **left front stance** (wen apkubi) and execute a **pulling high section uppercut** (dangkyo teokjireugi) with slow concentrated force.

5. Moving the left foot, turn 270° counterclockwise into **right front stance** (oreun apkubi) and execute a **single mountain block** (wesanteul makki). Look toward the left side of the body.

7a. Step the left foot in front of the right into **front cross stance** (apkoaseogi).

7b. Moving the right foot, step into **left front stance** (wen apkubi) execute a **single mountain block** (wesanteul makki). Look toward the right side of the body.

8. Without stepping, slowly pivot into **right front stance** (oreun apkubi) and execute a **pulling high section uppercut** (dangkyo teokjireugi) with slow concentrated force.

9. Moving the right foot, turn 90° counterclockwise into **right back stance** (oreun dwitkubi), executing a **double knife hand block** (sonnal momtongmakki).

10. Slide the left forward into **left front stance** (wen apkubi) and execute a **right straight middle punch** (momtong barojireugi).

11a. With the left foot fixed, execute a **right front kick** (oreunbal apchagi) then set the right foot down in its original position.

11b. Draw the left foot back into **right tiger stance** (oreun beomseogi) and execute a **right palm heel middle section block** (batangson momtongmakki).

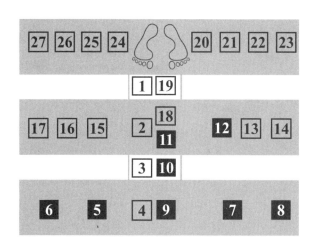

12. Moving the left foot, turn 90° counterclockwise into **left tiger stance** (wen beomseogi), and execute a **double knife hand block** (sonnal momtongmakki).

13a. With the right foot fixed, execute a **left front kick** (wenbal apchagi).

13b. Set the left foot down into **left front stance** (wen apkubi) and execute a **right straight middle punch** (momtong barojireugi).

14. Move the left foot toward the right into **left tiger stance** (wen beomseogi) and execute a **left palm heel block** (batangsonmakki).

17. Move the right foot toward the left into **right tiger stance** (oreun beomseogi) and execute a **right palm heel block** (batangsonmakki).

16b. Set the right foot down into **right front stance** (oreun apkubi) and execute a **left straight middle punch** (momtong barojireugi).

16a. With the left foot fixed, execute a **right front kick** (oreunbal apchagi).

15. Moving the left foot, turn 270° counterclockwise into **right tiger stance** (oreun beomseogi) and execute a **double knifehand block** (sonnal momtongmakki).

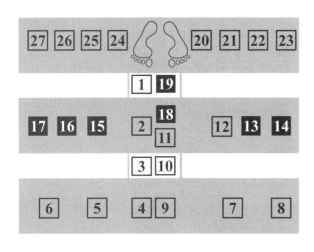

19a-b. Execute a **left front kick** (wenbal apchagi) followed immediately by a **right jump front kick** (oreunbal twio apchagi) with **kihap**.

18. Moving the left foot, turn 90° clockwise into **left back stance** (wen dwitkubi) and execute a **right augmented low section block** (kodureo arraemakki).

19d-e. With the feet fixed, execute a **double punch** (dubeon jireugi), punching first with the left hand and then with the right.

19c. After kicking, land in **right front stance** (oreun apkubi) and execute a **right inward middle block** (momtong anmakki).

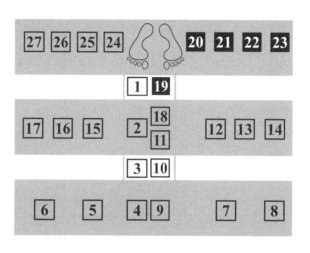

20. Moving the left foot, turn 270° into **right back stance** (oreun dwitkubi) and execute a **single knifehand middle section outward block** (hansonnal momtong bakkatmakki).

21. Slide the left foot forward into **left front stance** (wen apkubi) and execute a **right elbow strike** (oreun palkup dollyochigi).

22. With the feet fixed, execute a **right backfist strike** (oreun deungjumeok apchigi).

23. With the feet fixed, execute a **left reverse middle punch** (momtong bandaejireugi).

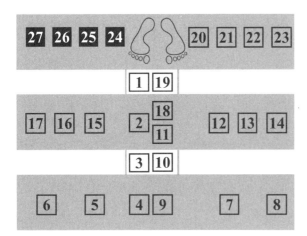

25. Slide the right forward into **right front stance** (oreun apkubi) and execute a **left elbow strike** (wen palkup dollyochigi).

24. Pivoting, turn 180° clockwise into **left back stance** (wen dwitkubi) and execute a **single knifehand middle section outward block** (hansonnal momtong bakkatmakki).

Moving the left foot, return to ready stance.

27. With the feet fixed, execute a **right reverse middle punch** (momtong bandaejireugi).

26. With the feet fixed, execute a **left backfist strike** (wen deungjumeok apchigi).

New Movements in Taegeuk Pal Jang

Front Cross Stance
Apkoaseogi

This is a transitional stance that allows you to move sideways between front stances or horseriding stances. One foot crosses in front of the other, with its small toe placed beside the sole of the fixed foot. The knees are bent and the shins form an X. Keep the feet as close together as possible.

Augmented Outward Middle Section Block
Kodureo Momtong Bakkatmakki

The palm of the blocking fist faces away from the body and the palm of the augmenting fist faces upward. The augmenting fist should be aligned on the same plane as the elbow of the blocking arm.

Single Mountain Block
Wesanteul Makki

The fist of the arm blocking the lower part of the body is held two fists' width from the thigh and the fist of the arm blocking the upper part of the body is aligned with the temple.

Augmented Low Section Block
Kodureo Arraemakki

The front hand is held about two fists' distance from the front thigh. The supporting hand is held in front of the solar plexus but does not touch the body. The wrists should be straight.

Pulling High Section Uppercut

Dangkyo Teokjireugi

Pulling the opponent's jaw with one hand, the other hand delivers an uppercut to the jaw. When completed the punching fist is at jaw height and the pulling fist is laid against the opposite shoulder. The pulling and punching motions should be simultaneous.

Index

About Dr. Sang H. Kim

Dr. Sang H. Kim (Sang-hwan Kim, 7th Dan) was born in Daegu, South Korea. He began Taekwondo training at the age of four. He taught Taekwondo at Trinity College from 1987 to 1994 and was a technical advisor for the Taekwondo programs at Wesleyan University and the University of Connecticut. He has spoken on Sports Philosophy, Fighting Strategy and Motivation in the US, Europe and Asia. He authored 14 books including the bestsellers *Ultimate Flexibility, Ultimate Fitness Through Martial Arts, Teaching: the Way of The Master, Taekwondo Kyorugi, Instructor's Desk Reference, Martial Arts After 40* and *1,001 Ways To Motivate Yourself and Others* (translated into more than 20 languages). He also starred in over 100 martial arts training films and DVDs including *Encyclopedia of Self-defense, Taegeuk Poomsae, Beginner Taekwondo, Ultimate Fitness for Martial Arts, Complete Kicking, Complete Sparring* and *Taekwondo Hand Skills.*

About Dr. Kyu Hyung Lee

Grandmaster Taekwondo 9th Degree Black Belt

Dr. Kyu Hyung Lee is one of the highest-ranking Taekwondo masters in the world and one of the most revered Poomsae instructors in the history of Taekwondo. He was the head of the 1988 Olympic Taekwondo Demonstration team and the Korean Team manager for the First World Taekwondo Poomsae Competition. From 1973 to 2005, he was the head of the internationally famous Midong Elementary School Demonstration team who has performed for royalty and heads of state around the world. From 1989 to 2005, he was the head of the Korean National Taekwondo Demonstration team. He holds a Ph.D. in physical education, 9th Dan black belt in Taekwondo and a WTF International Referee S (Special) class license. Currently he is a professor at Keimyung University in Daegu, South Korea.

Also Available from Turtle Press:
Fight Back
Winning on the Mat
Wrestle and Win
Fighting the Pain Resistant Attacker
Total Defense
Conditioning for Combat Sports
Kung Fu Grappling
Street Stoppers:
Sendo-Ryu Karate-do
Power Breathing
Throws and Takedowns
Drills for Grapplers
Vital Point Strikes
Groundfighting Pins and Breakdowns
Defensive Tactics
Secrets of Unarmed Gun Defenses
Point Blank Gun Defenses
Security Operations
Vital Leglocks
Boxing: Advanced Tactics and Strategies
Grappler's Guide to Strangles and Chokes
Fighter's Fact Book 2
The Armlock Encyclopedia
Championship Sambo
Complete Taekwondo Poomse
Martial Arts Injury Care and Prevention
Timing for Martial Arts
Strength and Power Training
Complete Kickboxing
Ultimate Flexibility
Boxing: A 12 Week Course
The Fighter's Body: An Owner's Manual
The Science of Takedowns, Throws and Grappling for Self-defense
Fighting Science
Martial Arts Instructor's Desk Reference
Solo Training
Solo Training 2
Fighter's Fact Book
Conceptual Self-defense
Martial Arts After 40
Warrior Speed
The Martial Arts Training Diary for Kids
Teaching Martial Arts
Combat Strategy
The Art of Harmony
Total MindBody Training
1,001 Ways to Motivate Yourself and Others
Ultimate Fitness through Martial Arts
Taekwondo Kyorugi: Olympic Style Sparring
Taekwondo Self-defense
Taekwondo Step Sparring
Complete Kicking

For more information:
Turtle Press
1-800-778-8785
e-mail: orders@turtlepress.com

http://www.turtlepress.com